TRAINING NEW AFTER-SCHOOL STAFF

WELCOME TO THE WORLD OF SCHOOL-AGE CARE!

by Roberta L. Newman

School-Age NOTES ● **Nashville Tennessee**

Roberta L. Newman has extensive experience as a director, trainer, and developer of curriculum materials for after-school programs. These materials include *Keys to Quality in School-Age Care* (video training), *Caring for Children in School-Age Programs* (written with Derry Koralek and Laura Colker) and *Building Relationships with Parents and Families in School-Age Programs*. She is also the author of *PAY ATTENTION!!! Answers to Common Questions About the Diagnosis and Treatment of Attention Deficit Disorder* (written with Craig B. Liden, M.D.) as well as a series of online courses on school-age care available through www.LearningOptions.org.

To schedule a workshop or staff training with Roberta contact:

Cape Charles Development Company
Eight Randolph Avenue
Cape Charles VA 23310
Telephone: 757-331-3151
E-mail: rlnccdc@aol.com

ISBN: 0-917505-13-1

Published by School-Age NOTES, P.O. Box 40205, Nashville TN 37204

CONTENTS

Introduction:
Tips for Directors on How to Use This Handbook

Training New After-School Staff: Welcome to the World of School-Age Care was created in response to requests from school-age directors across the country. Training more and more new staff at the beginning of each school year is a challenging task as the field grows. Most directors also find that they must continue to orient and train new staff throughout the year because of staff turnover.

In preparation for creating this handbook, School-Age NOTES and author Roberta Newman surveyed a sampling of school-age directors to identify what directors want new staff to understand and keep in mind as they begin their work. These directors shared many of the same interests and concerns. The topics explored in this handbook reflect what directors want staff to know about:

- understanding and responding to children's needs, interests and concerns
- building positive relationships with children
- planning for a successful first day
- providing safe, effective supervision
- developing and maintaining effective program rules and limits
- planning and implementing activities children will enjoy
- managing conflicts among children
- making parents feel welcome
  and more...

Training New After-School Staff is designed as a tool for school-age directors who want to provide new staff with important information and ideas for carrying out their responsibilities, but who have limited resources and time to devote to staff training. With this in mind, each section of the handbook provides interactive questions and scenarios which staff can work through independently. An *Answer Guide* provides possible answers and ideas for responding to selected scenarios.

Even though staff can use this handbook on their own, the handbook encourages them to share their answers to study questions and other ideas with a supervisor or a mentor. This is critically important, because many of the study questions ask new staff to think about how they could use the information in their own program. Rather than a standard answer guide for these questions, new staff will need supervisory feedback and suggestions from a supervisor, trainer, or designated experienced staff member. Otherwise, they may not succeed in using the tools in this handbook in ways which are best suited to your program.

Here are examples of ways to use *Training New After-School Staff* with new staff:

1)   *Train an individual staff member by assigning an experienced staff member to act as a mentor. Instruct the new staff member to complete one section of the handbook at a time and to discuss ideas and answers to the study questions with the assigned mentor before proceeding to the next section. Have the mentor set up a schedule which will allow new staff to complete the handbook before the first day, if possible.*

2)   *Train groups of new staff by assigning one section of the handbook at a time, giving a date and time you expect it to be completed. Then have a supervisor, trainer, or mentor meet with the group to facilitate discussion of the study questions and give suggestions and feedback.*

3)   *Conduct group training sessions based on the handbook. Have new staff work together to explore the topics and develop answers to the study questions during the training sessions.*

PART ONE:
School-Age Care: One of the Most Important Jobs You'll Ever Have!

What Is School-Age Care All About? A Look at an Emerging Profession.....

Congratulations! By accepting a position in a school-age program, you have joined thousands of others across the country who are playing a major, positive role in the lives of children and youth while they are out of school!

Your program may be sponsored by a youth organization, a school, a church or temple, a child care center, a government agency, or another community or business organization. Regardless of who sponsors your program, you and your co-workers have an opportunity to join with other child and youth advocates nationwide who are building the school-age field into an important, emerging profession.

This is an exciting time for school-age staff and school-age programs. Before you begin your work, let's take a brief look at what school-age care is all about, how the field has developed since the early 1970's, where it is going in the future, and how you can help shape its direction.

Changing Times and the Growing Need.....

As family life styles began to change and more women began to enter the workforce in the late 1960's, more and more school-age children and youth came home to empty homes after school. Children who wore a house key around their necks during the school day and went home alone after school were referred to as "latch-key" children. Increasing numbers of latch-key children found themselves in "self care" and supervised their own after-school activities.

Researchers found that latch-key children were often at risk for being harmed by others and by unsafe conditions in their home or neighborhood. Many latch-key children lacked the life skills, maturity, and judgment to be on their own. In addition, some research indicated that latch-key children were often bored, lonely, and depressed as they spent hours locked in their own homes. For many children, television was becoming the substitute for positive relationships with adults and friends.

Where We Are Now.....

Within a few years, concerned citizens and parents began to work together to increase the availability of high quality, affordable, accessible school-age programs in their communities. Since the 1970's, many communities have shared their experiences and knowledge with others across the nation. The box below highlights some of the important things you should know about how the field of school-age care is growing:

HOW THE FIELD OF SCHOOL-AGE CARE IS GROWING

- *Growing Public Awareness and Support for Programs.* Through the work of thousands of parents and child and youth advocates like you, public awareness of the out-of-school needs of school-age children and youth is growing. This translates into funding and support for school-age programs. Federal funding makes it possible for states and localities to provide financial assistance to low-income families needing school-age services, to make more programs available, and to improve the quality of programs. Private sector corporations are also supporting school-age care by providing funding for curriculum development and training, and assisting communities with program development.

- *Growing Emphasis on School-Age Care as a Profession.* Through local, state, and national networking and training efforts, school-age programs and staff members across the country are establishing school-age care as a viable profession. There is now a national organization dedicated to this effort—the **National School-Age Care Alliance (NSACA). NSACA** sponsors an annual national conference, supports and assists regions, states, and localities on a wide variety of school-age care issues and concerns. Many states and localities also sponsor annual school-age conferences and training opportunities. **NSACA** is working with other groups and organizations to explore the development of a **Credentialing System** for staff in school-age programs. You may join **NSACA** directly or, in many states, through your state **NSACA Affiliate** organization. Check out the **NSACA** web-site for more information (www.nsaca.org).

- *Growing Emphasis on Providing Quality Programs.* As a result of years of research and networking by school-age professionals, more and more communities are committed to providing **high quality school-age programs**. The **National School-Age Care Alliance (NSACA)** has adopted 36 standards which provide a baseline of quality for programs who are committed to bringing out the best in each child and youth they serve. Programs who want to achieve the standards of excellence provided by the standards may apply to participate in **NSACA's National System of Program Improvement and Accreditation.**

- *Growing Availability of Resource Materials for School-Age Programs.* As the number of school-age programs increases, the demand for resource materials on how to plan and implement quality programs is also increasing. There are now hundreds of books, videos, and other resources available to help school-age staff develop quality programs.

What Will I Gain from Working in a School-Age Program?
What Do I Have to Give?

*Those privileged to touch the lives of children and youth
should constantly be aware that their impact on a single child
may affect a multitude of others a thousand years from now.*

Anonymous

Do I have the "right stuff" to work with school-age children and youth?

Whether you work in a school-age program for a few months or for many years, you will leave a lasting impression on the lives of the children and youth for years to come. Your school-age program offers a daily opportunity to enrich the lives of children and youth.

As you get ready to take on your new responsibilities, it's a good idea to think about what it takes to be successful working with school-age children and youth. Listed below are some important characteristics which school-age directors often look for when hiring new staff.

Typical Characteristics of School-Age Staff with the "Right Stuff"

Place a check next to the characteristics you think describe you.
Then complete the worksheet on the next page.

_____ *I really **like school-age children and youth**.*

_____ *I have **good communication skills**. I'm a **good listener** and I try to **learn about** other people's ideas, interests, and concerns. I am **comfortable expressing my thoughts, opinions, and feelings without being sarcastic or hurtful to others**.*

_____ *I am **energetic** and like to be actively involved with children and youth.*

_____ *I am a **good observer**. I'm **alert** and **aware** of what's going on around me. I'm **sensitive** and **tuned-in** to the needs and traditions of other individuals and cultures.*

_____ *I know how to **solve problems**. I try to stay calm, think about what the problem is about, talk with others about possible solutions, and try to choose the best solution.*

_____ *I try to use **common sense**.*

_____ *I am good at **cooperating, planning, and working with others**; I'm a **team player**.*

_____ *I have a **good sense of humor**. Even if I don't laugh or joke a lot, I try to take things lightly and see the humor in a situation.*

_____ *I am **patient, understanding, and supportive** when working with others.*

_____ *I am **flexible**; when my plans aren't working, I'm willing to try something else.*

_____ *I am **reliable**; you can count on me to follow through when I make a commitment.*

_____ *I am a **positive thinker**; when faced with a challenge or difficulty, I try to be **resourceful and creative** - to think about what **I can do**, not what **I can't do**.*

_____ *Generally, **I feel good about myself**; I don't have problems which could make it difficult to work and play successfully with school-age children and youth.*

WORKSHEET: Identifying My Strengths and How I Want to Grow

It's unlikely that you checked all or even most of the characteristics in the "right stuff" box. Most new staff have some of the "right stuff" characteristics and need to work on others. The important thing to do is to identify your strengths (the items you checked) and the characteristics you may need to develop on the job (the items you did not check).

Use the form below to list three personal characteristics which you think make you a good match for the job as well as three personal characteristics you may need to work on. Share your list with your supervisor and talk about ways you can use your strengths to the maximum and improve in areas where you think you need to develop.

__Three Personal Characteristics Which Show I Have the "Right Stuff" for the Job.....__

1._____

Ideas I have for putting this characteristic to work in my school-age program:

2._____

Ideas I have for putting this characteristic to work in my school-age program:

3._____

Ideas I have for putting this characteristic to work in my school-age program:

__Three Personal Characteristics I Would Like to Strengthen or Develop.....__

1._____

Ideas I have for developing this characteristic:

2._____

Ideas I have for developing this characteristic:

3._____

Ideas I have for developing this characteristic:

How Can I Be a Positive Role Model for School-Age Children and Youth?

There is no doubt children and youth will see you as a role model. This means it's very important for you to be aware of what you say and do and how you present yourself. Here are examples of what you can do to be sure you are a *positive role model:*

- *Smile and show interest in children and youth by greeting them warmly every day.*
- *Use a respectful, polite tone of voice.*
- *Be a good listener.*
- *Exhibit patience and kindness in your interactions with others.*
- *Be clear about what you expect from children and youth.*
- *Show by your actions that you are enthusiastic about your work.*
- *Stay calm and collected during problems and emergencies.*
- *When problems occur, use a step-by-step approach to solving them.*
- *Use self-control and avoid yelling, name calling, sarcasm, and belittling people when you're angry.*
- *If you have a disagreement or problem with a co-worker, your supervisor, or a parent, work it out in private. Never discuss important concerns or confidential matters in front of children, youth, or their families.*
- *Dress appropriately for the work you do; wear clothing which is comfortable, clean, and allows you to move around freely. Avoid suggestive or tight clothing, high heeled shoes which might prevent you from moving quickly in an emergency, or clothing with printing which contains curse words or other disrespectful images and sayings.*

Another very effective way to be a role model for children and youth is to **share your special interests with them.** We all have **life skills** which school-age children might enjoy learning how to do. Think about some of the things you like to do which might be interesting to school-agers. Here are some examples of hobbies, skills, talents, and other special interests which can be appropriate to share with school-age children and youth:

- *Sports skills*
- *Acting, dancing, singing, playing a musical instrument*
- *Knitting, crocheting, sewing, embroidery, weaving, and other handicrafts*
- *Cooking*
- *Drawing, painting, cartooning, calligraphy and other artistic talents and skills*
- *Community service*
- *Woodworking*
- *Collecting*

WHAT I'VE LEARNED ABOUT THE FIELD OF SCHOOL-AGE CARE

In **PART ONE**, you explored the field of school-age care by:

- *Looking at how the field of school-age care got started and how it is growing and developing.*

- *Looking at some of the typical characteristics of staff who are successful in school-age programs.*

- *Thinking about how your own personal characteristics match up with the job.*

- *Exploring ideas for being a positive role model for school-age children and youth.*

Before moving on to the next section, take a few moments to think about how you feel about your new responsibilities working in a school-age program. Write down some of your thoughts below and share them with your supervisor. Make a plan for dealing with any potential problems or concerns.

1.   How do I think of my new position? As a **ROUTINE JOB**? As an **OPPORTUNITY TO JOIN AND HELP BUILD AN IMPORTANT PROFESSION**? As a **LEARNING EXPERIENCE**? As a chance to **HELP CHILDREN GROW AND LEARN?** Or as something else...............? How could my answer to this question affect the way I carry out my responsibilities?

2.   What are some ways I can connect my experiences in school-age care with my main personal goals and interests? What can I do to be sure this work is rewarding and fulfilling for me?

Now complete the following sentence openers:

Three things I can do every day to make sure I give my best to school-age children are.....

I think I can be a positive role model for school-age children and youth because.....

One personal interest, hobby, skill, or talent I think it would be appropriate to share with children in the program is.....

PART TWO:
Who Are School-Age Kids and What Do They Need from Me?

A Look at Characteristic Traits of School-Age Children and Youth.....

School-age children and youth are growing and changing in many different ways as they move through the years between ages 5 and 13. To be successful working with kids in out-of-school programs, it's important to keep their typical needs, interests, and characteristics in mind. One way to do this is to think about some of the main developmental tasks they are working on during these years. Here is a brief overview of some important tasks of school-agers, along with examples of how children might work on them in your school-age program.

They are growing physically. They need many opportunities for physical activity as well as time to rest, relax, and unwind. They want to challenge their bodies to learn new skills through sports, active games, and activities which allow them to use small muscles and develop fine motor skills. They need lots of fuel for their growing bodies and are often VERY HUNGRY! Newly emerging physical capabilities and characteristics may lead them to test out what they can do with their growing bodies. This often leads them to experiment and take risks. When physical needs aren't met, children sometimes exhibit behavior problems.

> **Seven-year-olds Simone and Keisha** do clapping games while they chant favorite rhymes. They work on learning new moves and try to go faster and faster.
>
> **Eight-year-olds Casey and David** want to go outside or to the gym when they arrive after school; they like to run and play active games with their friends before starting their homework.
>
> **Eleven-year-olds Samantha, Karin, and Hannah** are working on their rope-jumping skills. They keep track of their progress from day to day. When they get tired, they like to go to the art area where they are teaching themselves how to do calligraphy.

They are developing new thinking abilities and skills. They can use reasoning skills to solve problems. They like to categorize, investigate, experiment, and test out their ideas. They can plan, organize and make decisions about their own activities. Their increasing attention spans lead them to pursue activities which last for hours and continue the next day. They use their imaginations to think about people, places, and events beyond the immediate present. They can use thinking skills to explore questions about *right and wrong* and other moral issues.

Eight-year-old Ellen wants to be an airline pilot like her uncle. She likes to design model airplanes, fly kites, and read books about things that fly. She's amazed that migrating birds travel thousands of miles every year. She wonders what it would be like if people had wings.

Twelve-year-olds Sarah, Jeremy, and Cara are sitting in the quiet corner looking at a book about protecting the environment. They think it would be a good idea to organize a recycling center in the program and make a list of different things they could collect. They decide to start with aluminum cans because lots of people throw them on the ground in the neighborhood. They make a plan for getting other kids involved.

__They are developing social skills.__ They can use emerging communication skills to help them get along with others. Increasing language skills help them express opinions, ideas, and feelings in conversations with peers and adults. They like to work on projects and mutual interests together. Small and large group activities and sports and games provide opportunities for them to use and practice social skills such as listening, cooperating, problem solving, negotiating, compromising, and exercising self-control.

Six-year-olds Kevin, Jamal, and Jason are setting up a grocery store in the dramatic play area. They talk about how much to charge for each item and go to the art area where they work together to make signs to advertise the store. While making the signs, they talk about how to operate the store and what job each will do. All three boys want to be the check-out clerk and use the cash register. They decide to take turns. To decide who gets to be the check out clerk first, they write their names on a piece of paper and ask a staff member to pick out one of the papers.

Ten-year-olds Marie, Alishia, and Nicole love to dance. They think it would be great fun to have a dance club. They recruit other friends who like to dance and set up a meeting to plan their club.

__They are expanding their world beyond home and family.__ As their physical, social, and thinking skills increase, they want to use these skills to connect with the "real world." They are learning about the traditions and history of people from different backgrounds and cultures. They are working to make sense of the world as they experience interactions with peers and adults outside their own families. They are increasingly aware of community concerns and of happenings and events in the news. They want to make a difference in the world.

Nine-year-olds Monica and Rene heard about a family in their community whose house burned down over the weekend. The family is living in a homeless shelter temporarily. Their three school-age children lost all of their clothing and toys in the fire. Monica and Rene ask the school-age program staff if they could organize a drive to collect clothing and toys to help the children.

Eleven-year-olds Gunnar and Daniel have been learning about the disappearing rainforests in school. They are concerned about endangered species which may become extinct if the rainforests are destroyed. They want to write to the International Children's Rainforest program to find out what they could do to help save the rainforests.

They are moving toward competence. They are using their emerging physical, social, and thinking abilities to *get good at doing things*. They want to learn and practice new physical skills through sports, games, athletic skill clinics, fitness clubs, or individual activities like learning and performing yo-yo tricks. They like to learn new arts and crafts skills and techniques such as weaving, calligraphy, gimp, or origami. Complex games like chess help them increase their thinking skills. They like the challenge of developing teamwork through competitive and cooperative games. They feel a sense of accomplishment when they put on a talent show, raise money for a community project, harvest a garden or complete another big project successfully.

> **Five-year-olds Aaron, Wanika, and Rachel** are working with a staff member to harvest herbs they have been growing in a window garden over the past few months. They will use some of them to season a soup they are making together. They will dry some of the herbs to use in other cooking projects.
>
> **Twelve-year-old Mason** has perfected 10 magic tricks. He's performing them tonight at a parent meeting.

They are experiencing many new thoughts and feelings. Many new thoughts and feelings emerge as school-age children and youth experience physical, social, and intellectual development. They need many opportunities to explore, sort out, and express these thoughts and feelings as a sense of self is developing. They seek out opportunities for creative expression through activities such as music, dance, writing, and art. Activities related to science and sports can also serve as vehicles for expression of new ideas, thoughts, and feelings.

> **Nine-year-old Astrid** is enjoying learning about her family's Swedish traditions and folklore. She hopes to visit Sweden someday. She has seen pictures of the farm her grandmother lived on in Sweden and thinks about what it would be like to grow up in Sweden. She likes to make pictures of Swedish farmhouses and writes poems about mystical elves who live in Swedish barns.
>
> **Ten-year-olds Jerrel and Damon** are feeling proud of their new basketball skills. They have designed a routine of the things they can do and plan to give a demonstration for other kids in the program.

They are moving toward independence. As their new capabilities increase, they want to use them to become more independent. They seek out opportunities to do things for themselves, to direct their own interests, to choose their favorite activities, and to be reliable and assume responsibilities. They enjoy being resourceful and like to take on leadership roles.

> **Five-year-olds Kaitlyn and Joey** volunteer to be snack helpers. Every day, they help set up the snack area with cups, napkins, and utensils. They also help decorate the tables and pick out background music to create a pleasant atmosphere during snack.
>
> **Seven-year-olds Jerome and Ben** love to play board games. They get upset when they can't find all the pieces to their favorite games. They decide to make a poster for the game area reminding their friends to put games away when they're finished playing with them.

The important thing to remember about the characteristic needs and tasks of school-agers is that children are *"works in progress."* They are just beginning to grow in some areas and may be quite advanced in others. And each child experiences the developmental tasks in a unique way. Whatever task they are working on, school-age children thrive when staff tune in to their needs and provide them with appropriate support, help, and guidance.

What You Can Do. Look back at the examples of developmental tasks provided in the box after each area. Select *one example* and think about what you could do to provide support, help, guidance, or encouragement to children in the example. Link your ideas to the task they are working on. Write your ideas below; share them with your supervisor.

*Child(ren) in the example:*_____

*Developmental Task:*_____

Ideas I have for providing support, help, guidance, or encouragement to these children:

_____

_____

_____

A Look at Individual Differences Among School-Age Children and Youth and How You Can Support Them......

While school-age children and youth have many things in common, they are also different from each other in many ways:

They have different INTERESTS. They like to choose what they will do in school-age programs. To support different interests, staff can provide a mixture of activities such as:

- *board and table games*
- *arts and crafts*
- *reading and other quiet activities*
- *dramatic play*
- *music and dance*
- *blocks and construction*
- *science and nature*
- *math enrichment activities*
- *homework support*
- *group sports and active games*
- *individual physical activities (e.g. hula hoops, jump roping)*
- *cooking*
- *special interest clubs and community service projects*
- *field trips to places of interest in the community*
- *visits from people with interesting talents and skills to share*

They have different ABILITIES, TALENTS, SKILLS, and LEARNING STYLES. Some children excel at physical activities. Some have a talent for music and dancing. Some enjoy reading and writing poems and stories. Some are artistic. Some have leadership skills. Some have a knack for getting along with others and being a team player. Here are some ways staff can help children make the most of their unique capabilities:

- *Observe children closely and plan activities which match their abilities.*
- *Ask children about things they really like to do and try to include them in the program.*
- *Ask children what they think they're good at as well as what they don't feel good at.*
- *Encourage children to try new things.*
- *Provide support and encouragement for children who want to work on difficult challenges.*
- *Help children find resources and ideas for building on their strengths.*

**They come from different BACKGROUNDS.** Children in school-age programs come from many different cultures, races, socio-economic groups. Each family represented in your program has its own beliefs, values, traditions, and life style. It is also likely that many different family structures are represented in your program. Some families may be headed by a single parent. Others may be families where both parents work outside the home. There may also be families headed by a foster parent or by a family member such as a grandparent or an aunt or uncle. Here are examples of ways staff and programs can support _diversity_ among children and families:

- _Encourage children to tell you about their family traditions and customs._

- _Invite family members to visit and share favorite recipes, songs, dances, games, or other family traditions and favorite activities._

- _Provide books, pictures, and posters portraying people from different backgrounds in many different roles._

- _Provide dress up clothing, foods, music and dance activities which reflect different national and cultural backgrounds and traditions._

- _Help parents get to know each other - introduce them to each other, display pictures of parents and their children, provide a bulletin board where parents can share information._

- _Be aware of parents and children whose primary language is not English - talk to your supervisor about ways you can help them connect with the program._

**They have differences in TEMPERAMENT.** Research has shown that each of us is born with traits and tendencies which influence how we process and interact with the world. Here are some examples of differences in temperament among people (both children and adults):

- _Some have a HIGH ACTIVITY LEVEL; others tend to be LESS ACTIVE._

- _Some have a tendency to be SHY AND WITHDRAW FROM NEW EXPERIENCES; others are OUTGOING and may even be risk-takers._

- _Some are ADAPTABLE; others find it DIFFICULT TO ADJUST TO CHANGE._

- _Some are very SENSITIVE to light, heat, sound, touch. Others are LESS SENSITIVE to things in the environment. (SENSITIVITY may also relate to how we respond to criticism and negative feedback from others.)_

- _Some tend to be very PERSISTENT; others may GIVE UP EASILY when faced with a challenge or learning a new skill._

- _Some may tend to be IMPULSIVE and ACT WITHOUT THINKING; others may be REFLECTIVE and THINK THINGS THROUGH BEFORE ACTING._

- _Some may be EASILY DISTRACTED and have DIFFICULTY FOCUSING ATTENTION on activities; others may be able to FILTER OUT DISTRACTIONS in order to STAY FOCUSED._

- *Some may have INTENSE REACTIONS to things which happen in their environment; others may RESPOND CALMLY AND EVENLY.*

- *Some tend to be POSITIVE IN MOOD; others tend to be NEGATIVE IN MOOD.*

Because temperamental traits and tendencies are inborn, it is important to be aware of them and think about the best way to manage them. Here are some things staff can do:

- *Observe children closely. Ask yourself if behavior you are seeing seems related to temperamental traits and tendencies. If your answer is yes, think about the best way to respond to children or redirect them.*

- *Anticipate potential behavior problems which may be related to temperament and intervene before the situation deteriorates.* **Example:** A child who is highly active, tends to act without thinking, and often has intense reactions to things is getting very excited and "revved up" during a highly competitive kickball game. *An effective way to respond would be to 1) point out to the child he (or she) is getting very excited, 2) encourage the child to take a break and get a drink of water.* This can help the child calm down and stay in control. **Note:** *You might also ask yourself whether the physical activities offered place too much emphasis on intense competition. A solution might be to offer a better mix of competitive and low-keyed games.*

WHAT I'VE LEARNED ABOUT SCHOOL-AGE CHILDREN AND YOUTH

In **PART TWO,** you learned about the needs of school-age children and youth by:

- *Looking at characteristic ways that children and youth grow and change during the school-age years.*

- *Looking at individual differences among school-age children and youth - differences in interests, abilities, talents, skills, learning styles, backgrounds, and temperament.*

- *Exploring things you can do to support school-age children's characteristic needs and individual differences.*

Before moving on to the next section, read the following scenarios and use the space provided to answer the questions which follow them. Share your answers with your supervisor. **Note:** You may want to compare your answers with possible answers provided in the **Answer Guide** at the end of the book.

Scenario One. Kyle, Mario, and Tommy are playing with Lego® blocks. Six-year-old Kyle has been sitting at a table by himself. He is using the Lego® blocks to make cars and trucks. Before starting to build, he makes piles of different pieces and counts the wheels to figure out how many cars he can make. Kyle begins to have trouble manipulating some of the pieces. Another child offers to help him, but he says, "I want to figure out how to do this by myself."

Two nine-year-olds, Mario and Tommy, are sitting on a rug nearby. They decide to make a huge Lego® city. Mario wants to start by building a skyscraper like one he saw on the news last night; he tells Tommy it needs to have a strong foundation so it won't fall down in an earthquake. They talk about the best way to make a skyscraper which won't fall down. Then they experiment with different ways to make their structure stable and sturdy. When the skyscraper is finished, they work together for over an hour building more skyscrapers, office buildings connected with bridges and walkways, apartment buildings, and streets with small shops. They decide it's important for cities to have some outdoor places for people to eat lunch and meet friends. So they move some of their buildings to make room for parks. They stand back and look at their model city and Mario says "It looks awesome! I'd like to live in that fancy apartment!" "Not me!" says Tommy. "I'd rather live in a house with a yard. I'd drive to work every day. Maybe tomorrow we could make some cars for the parking lot. Let's ask if we can save the city so we can use it again tomorrow."

- *What developmental tasks are the different boys in the scenario working on while they play with Lego® blocks?*

- *What are some ways you could support, help, guide, or encourage each of the children in this scenario?*

Scenario Two. Haley and Jasmine, both 12-year-olds, wander around the art area and watch some children at a table who are gluing fabric pieces, yarn, and other collage materials on pre-cut figures of people. They're making dresses and other outfits for the figures and using the yarn to create hair. Haley says to Jasmine: "Those people look like gingerbread men; that's not how people look! I want to be a fashion designer when I grow up and fashion designers don't use models like that! Come on, let's get some paper and colored pencils and I'll design an outfit for you. I'm good at drawing people that look like models in magazines." Jasmine says, "Great, I'll sit over here and you can pretend I'm a model. Design something cool I can wear to a party. I love bright colors!"

- *What developmental tasks are Haley and Jasmine working on in this scenario?*

- *What are some ways you could support, help, guide, or encourage them?*

Scenario Three. Ten-year-olds Maria and Belinda are visiting together in the Library Corner. Maria says, "You know, last year I had a lot more fun here. They let me be the helper in the art area and I taught the other kids how to do lots of things. But the person who used to help us with art left and no one asks me to help anymore." "What kind of stuff can you do?" says Belinda. "Well, I'm really creative, you know," says Maria. "I've learned how to do neat things like origami, weaving, paper mache, and I'm really good at making paper flowers. My grand-mother helps me learn things. She travels a lot and brings me things from different countries. That's how I learned how to make paper flowers. She brought a whole bunch back to me from Mexico last year when she visited our relatives. She even gave me a book on how to make the flowers. I have them all over my bedroom at home." "So, could you teach me how to make them?" asks Belinda. "Sure, but I don't know if we have the stuff we need to do it."

- *What developmental tasks are Maria and Belinda working on in this scenario?*

- *What ideas do you have for helping Maria make the most of her interests, abilities, talents, and family background during the program?*

Scenario Four. A group of five- and six-year-olds have organized their own volleyball game. They've been watching the summer Olympics and think volleyball looks like a lot of fun. But they're having lots of trouble. They can't serve the ball. They can't hit the ball over the net. Every time someone hits the ball, it rolls down a small hill and all the kids run to see who can catch it first. Then they come back and start again. One of the kids says "This isn't as much fun as it looks on TV."

- *What ideas do you have for helping, supporting, and guiding children in this scenario?*

Scenario Five. Nine-year-old Kendra stands by watching a group of girls who are doing "Double Dutch" rope jumping. She chants the rhymes they are using quietly to herself and fidgets around with her feet. She doesn't make a move to join the group. No one seems to notice her except for Jeremy who passes by and says "What's the matter, don't you have any friends?" Kendra calls Jeremy a name, takes a swing at him, but misses. Then she moves farther away from the group.

- *What temperamental characteristics could be related to Kendra's behavior?*

- *What ideas do you have for helping her get involved in the jump rope activity?*

Scenario Six. Six-year-old Sammy runs in the program door. He throws his bookbag toward his cubby and misses. When he sees his friend, Ben, he forgets about it. He dashes over to the area where his group is getting together for a meeting and throws himself down next to Ben. As soon as Sammy sits down, he pokes Ben, starts pulling on his shirt, and tries to get him into a friendly wrestling match. Ben tells him to stop. Sammy turns his attention for a moment to the staff member making announcements, but quickly interrupts her, saying "When can we go outside? I'm ready now!"

- *What temperamental characteristics could be related to Sammy's behavior?*

- *What changes to you think the staff could make to help Sammy connect with the program in a positive way?*

PART THREE:
How I Can Get Off to a Good Start My First Day at Work

One of the most important things you can do on your first day of work is to keep the needs of school-age children and youth in mind. The information you explored in **PART ONE** and **PART TWO** will help you do this. In addition, before you begin to work, you need to be well-informed about your school-age program, about your specific responsibilities, and have some ideas for making positive connections with children right from the start.

Learning All About Your School-Age Program.....

Although school-age programs across the country have many things in common, each program has its own unique structure, style, and operating guidelines. Your program director will provide you with important information about your program through pamphlets, guidebooks or manuals, orientation packets, and/or meetings. Make it a priority to become familiar with this information. Never be afraid to ask questions about things you don't understand.

Listed below are things that many school-age directors want all staff to know about their programs before the first day of work. Place a check next to topics which you fully understand in relation to your program.

I understand this topic	_Important Information About My School-Age Program_
_____	**Program mission, philosophy, goals, objectives**
_____	**Behavior management policies and procedures**
_____	**Release policies and procedures (to whom children may be released and under what circumstances)**
_____	**Fire drill procedures**
_____	**Medical emergency procedures**
_____	**Weather-related emergency procedures**
_____	**Touch policy (defining appropriate ways of touching children and youth)**
_____	**Child abuse reporting policies and procedures**
_____	**Safety and health standards and checklists**

Learning About Your Job Responsibilities.....

In addition to learning about your program, it's very important to fully understand *your specific job responsibilities* before the first day. In the box below, place a check next to topics which you fully understand about your new position.

I understand this topic	*Important Information About My Responsibilities*
_____	**My overall job description**
_____	**My program's personnel policies and procedures (e.g. attendance policies, leave policies, payroll policies, grievance policies, termination policies, benefits, etc.)**
_____	**Program Area(s) where I will be working**
_____	**My responsibility for planning and leading activities**
_____	**Where I can find resources for planning**
_____	**My responsibility for gathering resources and arranging the program environment**
_____	**My responsibility for supervising children's safety, play, and learning experiences**
_____	**Names of children I am responsible for supervising**
_____	**Names of co-workers who will be working with me**
_____	**Who I report to - who to ask for help when I need it**
_____	**My responsibility for participating in training activities**
_____	**My responsibility for interacting with parents**
_____	**Additional responsibilities I may have**

After completing the previous two checklists, review the information provided by your program on any topics you are unclear about. Make a list of any topics which are still confusing. Then, meet with your supervisor or an assigned mentor to clarify any remaining questions or concerns. Be sure to ask whether your program has any *additional policies or procedures which you should know about.*

Tips for Building a Positive Relationship with Children from the First Moment.....

Staff who are successful in school-age programs work hard at building positive relationships with all children and youth. Relationship building starts the first time you interact with a child. Listed below are some ideas for reaching out to children and youth in your program on the first day of service.

- Greet each child with a friendly smile.

- Use name tags to help you learn children's names; be sure to use names when talking with children as soon as possible.

- Learn at least one strategy you can use the first day to get children's attention, gather them into a group, or prepare for a transition to another activity or area. Here is an example of an effective attention getting strategy:

  *In a quiet voice say, "If you can hear me, tap your head." (Begin lightly tapping your own head. Kids standing close by are likely to begin tapping their heads right away.) Continue tapping your head and repeat the request again, "If you can hear me, tap your head." (A few more kids will join in.) Continue tapping your head and repeating the phrase until you have everyone's attention. **Variations:** Change the request each time: "If you can hear me, clap twice.....touch your toes.....snap your fingers..... say Oh yeah!.....etc. (See **School-Age NOTES Resource Catalog** for other resources with ideas for bringing groups together.)*

- Express enthusiasm and excitement about what you and the children will be doing together. Give them a "tour" of the environment. Review the schedule of activities. Invite them to tell you about things they like to do.

- Set a positive tone: Talk briefly with children about how they would like to be treated and invite suggestions about ways everyone can get along. Stress principles and values such as listening to the ideas and concerns of others, sharing, cooperating, showing respect, politeness, kindness, and patience.

- Talk with children about <u>your program's established rules and limits, stressing safety issues.</u> Invite children to give suggestions about other rules and limits which would keep everyone safe and happy. Write down their ideas - keep them brief, to the point, and help children state them positively. (For example, instead of "No mean teasing," suggest "Be kind to each other.") Post children's ideas in a visible spot as a reminder.

- If you are responsible for planning or leading games or activities, be prepared with all resources you will need and make a plan for how you will get the activity started. (A later section contains suggestions for activity planning and preparation.)

- Be sure you know how to use your program's system for keeping track of children's whereabouts. REMEMBER YOU ARE ACCOUNTABLE!

- Be sure you know who each child may be released to when it's time to leave the program. Check release policies and forms in advance.

WHAT I'VE LEARNED ABOUT GETTING OFF TO A GOOD START ON MY FIRST DAY

In **PART THREE,** you have explored ideas for getting off to a good start in your school-age program by:

- *Identifying what I need to know in advance about my school-age program.*

- *Identifying what I need to know about my specific responsibilities.*

- *Thinking about what I can do to build a positive relationship with children and youth from the first moment they walk in the door.*

Before moving on to the next section, take some time to think about what steps you will take to ensure you have a successful first day with school-age children and youth in your program. Keep in mind *1) what you know about the characteristic needs of school-agers, 2) what you know about your program, and, 3) your specific job responsibilities*. Use the space below to write down a plan for the first day. Before the first day, review your plan with your supervisor and/or an assigned mentor or co-worker and make any needed changes.

SPECIFIC THINGS I NEED TO REMEMBER WHEN PLANNING MY FIRST DAY:
(Note: *If you are joining a program which is already in full swing, be sure to think about how to relate to policies, rules, and procedures which are already in place. Talk with a co-worker and make a plan about the best way to introduce yourself and get to know the children.):*

MY PLAN FOR MY FIRST DAY AT WORK IN MY SCHOOL-AGE PROGRAM:

How I will greet and get to know children:

How I will let children know about established program policies and procedures and other things they need to know:

Things I will do to help children get involved in the program: (e.g. prepare the environment, lead an activity, play a "get to know you" game, etc.)

PART FOUR:
What Are Some Common DO's and DON'Ts for Staff in School-Age Programs?

Things I Should Always Keep in Mind When Working with School-Age Children.....

In a recent survey, **School-Age NOTES** invited a group of school-age directors from around the country to identify *the most important things they want staff to know and keep in mind* when working in their programs. Many of them stressed the importance of enjoying children, having fun with children, and keeping them safe. A summary list of their responses appears below.

<u>Important Things School-Age Directors Want Staff to Keep in Mind</u>

- *Smile and have fun with the children while you keep them safe.*

- *Be nurturing and understanding.*

- *Share your enthusiasm and enjoyment of being with children.*

- *Safety is your #1 goal!* (e.g. Be alert and aware of children's whereabouts at all times. Provide a safe environment by checking regularly for safety hazards. Remove hazards from the environment. Set safe boundaries while children are playing active games. Be sure children are always under appropriate supervision. Be sure children are only re-leased to authorized persons. Talk with your supervisor and co-workers about other ways to keep children safe.)

- *Remember you are a powerful role model for children.* They notice everything you say and do and may copy you later!

- *Respect children. Be concerned about their emotional well-being.* Remember the best way to <u>get respect</u> is to <u>extend respect</u>.

- *Always keep the needs of children in mind.* (See PART TWO.)

- *Be involved with children. Be a DOER, not a WATCHER.* Remember that <u>supervision</u> and <u>interaction</u> are the two most important keys in working with children. Always see the "Whole Picture" even when working one-on-one or with a small group. (If Monica, Suzelle, and

Gena ask you to turn one end of the rope for "Double Dutch" rope jumping, join them as long as you are sure other children are safely occupied and you can keep an eye on everyone. Stay alert to what's going on around you—be sure other children aren't getting into a conflict, or climbing unsafely on the monkey bars. Enjoy the rope-jumping activity, but after awhile, look for another child who might like to turn the rope so that you can interact with other children who may need your help or attention.)

- *Talk with children—find out what's on their minds.* (e.g. If nine-year-old Gail is wandering aimlessly, try asking: "If you could do anything you wanted right now, what would it be?")

- *Remember that children are basically good; yet, some of their choices may not be.* One of your main goals is to help them learn about making good choices. (e.g. If ten-year-old Kevin wants to test his physical abilities by jumping off the top row of bleachers in the gym, be sure to intervene immediately. Tell Kevin you know he likes jumping, but that you can't let him jump from the bleachers because he could get hurt. Then, redirect him to another activity where he can challenge his physical capabilities safely— create an obstacle course, a space for broad jumping, or involve him in jump roping activities.)

- *Always follow program policies.*

- *Be ON TIME and be at work REGULARLY.* Always call when you won't be there—the children, the parents, and your co-workers are COUNTING ON YOU!

What I Should Avoid Doing When Working with School-Age Children.....

The same survey which asked school-age directors what they want staff to keep in mind also asked directors what they want staff to avoid doing if at all possible. A summary of directors' responses to this question is below.

As a School-Age Director, I Want School-Age Staff to Avoid

- *Leaving children alone - unsupervised.*

- *Using negative discipline. (*e.g. "put downs," yelling at children, getting into power plays with children, using sarcasm and ridicule to make children feel bad, denying food as punishment, being condescending.)

- *Using inappropriate language.* (e.g. "street talk," slang, curse words)

- *Role modeling inappropriate behavior.* (e.g. being argumentative; displaying anger and frustration by shouting or throwing things; being rude or disrespectful to children, co-workers, parents, or supervisors; wearing inappropriate or suggestive clothing)

- *Calling children "honey," "sweetheart," or "baby," instead of calling them by name.*

- *Failing to talk with children.*

- *Jumping to conclusions about a problem, making assumptions about what children want and need without asking them.*

- *Assuming children can take care of all disputes by themselves.*

- *Lack of involvement with children and lack of enthusiasm (e.g. standing back passively and "supervising" the group, chatting with co-workers instead of interacting with children)*

- *Taking over - failing to let children direct their own activities when they are able and willing to do so.*

- *Applying program rules, limits, and consequences <u>inconsistently.</u>*

- *Discussing personal issues with children - sharing details about their social life. (e.g. stories about staff member's boyfriends, parties, etc.)*

- *Touching children inappropriately. (e.g. having children sit on laps, hugging children tightly, kissing children).* **Note:** <u>Be sure you are aware of your program's Touch Policy.</u>

- *Being alone with children.* **Note:** <u>In some programs, this may be acceptable under certain circumstances. Be sure to find out about your program's policy concerning if or when you may be alone with children.</u>

- *Eating children's snack.* **Note:** <u>In some programs, this may be encouraged as part of family style dining. Be sure to check your program's policy.</u>

- *Giving children rides in personal vehicles on field trips or other occasions.*

- *Being late to work or absent from work frequently or without notification and explanation.*

- *Coming unprepared to lead an activity, game, or club*

- *Ignoring parents—failing to greet them, call them by name, talk with them about their child's experiences and their day.*

- *Being rude to parents or upsetting them unnecessarily.*

Training New After-School Staff

WHAT I'VE LEARNED ABOUT THE DO'S AND DON'TS FOR SCHOOL-AGE STAFF.

In **PART FOUR**, you have thought about the "do's and don'ts" for school-age staff by:

- *Exploring things school-age directors want their staff members to keep in mind at all times.*

- *Exploring things school-age directors want their staff members to avoid doing if at all possible.*

Before moving on to the next section, review the "do's and don'ts" for school-age staff in this section and think about how they relate to your program and your responsibilities. To help you do this, complete each of the sentences below. Review your answers with your supervisor. Make changes and ask for help and advice if needed.

- *Based on what I know about school-age children and <u>my school-age program</u>, the THREE MOST IMPORTANT THINGS I will keep in mind when working with school-agers are:*

  1._____

  2._____

  3._____

- *One thing I might need to be reminded to do when working with school-agers is:*

  _____

- *Something I'm not sure how to do when working with school-agers is:*

  _____

  _____

- *I'm not sure why it is important to avoid doing the following things when working with school-agers:*

  _____

  _____

- *I may need reminders or help to <u>AVOID</u> doing the following things when working with school-agers:*

  _____

  _____

30

PART FIVE:
Developing and Implementing Program Rules and Guidelines

Working with School-Age Children to Set Rules and Limits.....

As school-age children grow and change and interact with each other, they need to know what is acceptable and what is not acceptable. If your program has an established "code of conduct" it's important to share this with children on the first day. Most quality school-age programs recognize that pre-established guidelines are only a starting point. They know that children and youth are much more likely to "buy-in" and live by rules and limits if they have a chance to shape them.

A good way to begin a rule-making session, is to ask children why they think rules are needed and how rules can help us. Then work with children to make a list of the different things they think it would be important to have rules about. As children share their ideas, it's likely that they will identify many of the same topics you and your program think are important. They will probably suggest the kinds of things listed in the box below:

Examples of Things to Have Rules About:

- staying safe
- staying healthy
- treating each other with fairness, kindness, and respect
- getting along with each other
- respecting people's privacy
- sharing games and equipment
- respecting and protecting personal property
- respecting and protecting program materials, equipment, and facilities

---

Training New After-School Staff

When children have listed all their ideas, add any other topics you think should be included based on what you know about school-age children and about your program. Talk about each topic to be sure everyone agrees it's important. If your list is long, combine related topics. (This will help you avoid creating too many rules which can be confusing and hard to remember.) Then, involve children in a rule-making session, using the guidelines in the box below.

Guidelines for Rule-Making with School-Age Children and Youth

- _Look at each topic you identified and come up with a rule or guideline which could support the topic_ (e.g. A rule related to respecting people's privacy might be: "Keep your hands to yourself." A rule about getting along with each other might be: "If you have a problem, talk it out." A rule about staying safe might be: "Always wear goggles at the woodworking bench.")

- _State rules clearly and simply._ (e.g. "Wash your hands before eating and after using the bathroom.")

- _State rules positively._ (e.g. "Walking is the speed limit indoors," instead of "No running." "Use polite words," instead of "No swearing." Stating rules positively helps children focus their attention on what it means to DO THE RIGHT THING. It provides a course of action.)

- _Create only as many rules as you need to have the program run smoothly; try to generalize and establish a few basic guidelines which apply throughout the program._ (e.g. "Put things away when you're finished using them." "Use equipment properly; ask for help if you don't know how.")

- _Establish specialized rules for specific program areas if needed._ (e.g. In the board and table games area: "Return game pieces to the right box." "Return games to the shelf when finished." "Play by the rules." "Ask before you join a game in progress.")

Helping Children Take Responsibility for Their Actions.....

Involving children and youth in establishing rules and limits is the first step in getting them to "buy-in" and live by the rules. But it's important not to stop there. In order for program rules and limits to have **credibility**, children need to know what will happen if the rules are broken; they need to know the rules will be applied consistently and fairly, and **what the consequences will be** if they are broken. Ask them to look at the rules they have helped to shape and brainstorm some ideas about what should happen if the rules aren't followed.

As you talk with children, keep in mind these two types of consequences: **Natural Consequences** and **Logical Consequences**. _Natural Consequences_ happen as a direct result of an action. Here are some examples of _Natural Consequences_:

32

- If a child breaks the rule that says "*Keep your arms inside the bus,*" the child may suffer an injury as a natural consequence of putting his arm outside the bus.

- If a child regularly breaks the rule "*Use kind words*," the child may lose friends as a natural consequence of mean-spirited teasing and taunting.

- If a child breaks the rule that says "*Stay on the sidewalk*," the child may be hit by a car as a natural consequence of running out into the street.

- If a child doesn't observe the rule that says "*Wash hands before eating,*" the child may get sick.

As you can see, *Natural Consequences* can be disastrous for children if they are allowed to play out to their conclusion. As a staff member, it's important to anticipate any dangerous natural consequences which could occur if children break the rules, set up systems which make it easy for children to follow the rules, and take steps to intervene and guide children **before the rule is broken**. This is especially important when children's safety and well-being are at stake. No child should have to lose an arm in order to learn the importance of keeping his or her arms inside the bus windows!

Logical Consequences can be used very effectively to help children learn to accept responsibility for their actions. We can decide on many *Logical Consequences* in advance and let children know what will happen if a rule is broken.

Logical Consequences are directly related to what the rule is about. It would not be a *Logical Consequence* to tell a child who has been throwing sand at other children that he may not be in the Magic Club tomorrow. Sand throwing and participation in the Magic Club are not logically connected.

It's also important to keep things in balance. For example, if a child who usually picks up after himself forgets to put away the checkers game once, it would not be logical to ban the child from the board and table games area for a month. On the other hand, if a child continually ignores the rules about putting games away **after being reminded**, it would be logical to tell the child she may not use the board games for the rest of the day. *Immediate, short-term, logical consequences* are usually the most effective way to encourage children to take responsibility for their actions. Here are some examples of helping children take responsibility for their actions through reminders and effective *Logical Consequences:*

- If children break the rule *"Treat program materials with respect"* by throwing clay at the wall in the art area, *remind them of the rule and what they are allowed to do with clay.* Before continuing their play, have them work together to clean up the mess. Tell them they may continue to use the clay ONLY if they use it properly. If they begin to throw clay again, an *immediate, short-term logical consequence* would be to tell the children they may not use the clay for the rest of the day.

- If a child breaks the rule *"Be a good sport and always play safe"* by throwing a baseball bat in the air when he strikes out, *take action immediately.* Stay calm; move the child away from the group. Encourage him to "cool off " for a few minutes. Then, *remind* the child of the rule to be a good sport and always play safe. Tell the child you cannot allow him to throw his bat because someone could get hurt. If this is the first time the child has exhibited this behavior, a *short-term logical consequence* would be to have the child sit out for one or two "at bats" until he regains self-control. When he re-enters the game, give another *reminder* of the rule to "be a good sport and always play safe." If this child continues to have trouble living by the rule to be a good sport and always play safe, you may need to talk with your supervisor or co-workers about what else you need to do.

- If a child breaks the rule *"Use polite words"* by swearing at another child who wants to wear the same dress-up clothes, give the child a *reminder* of the rule for using polite words to talk through problems. If the child continues to use inappropriate language, a *short-term logical consequence* could be to tell her she must leave the dramatic play area for the afternoon.

Listed below are examples of things you can do to help children live by program rules and accept responsibility for their actions when rules and limits are broken or ignored.

Examples of Things Staff Can Do To Help Children Abide by Program Rules and Accept Responsibility for Their Actions

- *Involve children in setting program rules and limits.*

- *Involve children in making posters which list program rules and limits. Display posters in visible places in your program.*

- *Give children positive reminders about rules and limits. Talk with your co-workers about how many reminders or warnings you want to give before imposing a consequence. Remember that consequences for breaking safety rules may need to be imposed more quickly than consequences for failing to use quiet voices or forgetting to put things away.*

- *Use positive guidance techniques to help children follow rules and limits. For example:*

  * Redirect children to another activity or another area if they are having trouble following the rules.

  * Make it easy for children to follow the rules. For example, if you want children to take good care of equipment and supplies, be sure items are in good condition to begin with, provide adequate storage, and display items neatly and attractively.

  * Remove objects or equipment which children are not allowed to use.

* Stay close to children who may have a hard time remembering the rules or controlling their tempers.

* Help children pace themselves. For example, if children are becoming overly tired, anxious, or frustrated during an activity, encourage them to take a break or try something else for awhile.

- *Talk with children about possible consequences if rules are broken.*

- *Refrain from using harsh punishments as consequences when children break the rules. For example:*

    * NEVER withhold food as a consequence.

    * NEVER deny a child the right to tend to personal needs (going to the bathroom, getting a drink of water).

    * NEVER belittle, ridicule, humiliate, or scream at children as a consequence. CONTROL YOUR OWN ANGER and comment on what the child has done - not on who the child is.

- *Remember to keep in mind individual differences among children.* (e.g. children who are impulsive, intense, or highly distractible may need more help and support to abide by the rules)

- *Be consistent and fair in your application of rules and limits. Don't "play favorites."*

- *Apply consequences effectively when rules are broken or ignored.*

- *Remember that rules may need to be changed, added, or dropped as children grow and change. Meet frequently with children to "rule review" sessions. Get rid of any rules you no longer need. Add others.*

WHAT I'VE LEARNED ABOUT DEVELOPING AND IMPLEMENTING PROGRAM RULES AND GUIDELINES

In **PART FIVE,** you have explored ideas for developing and implementing program rules and guidelines for school-age programs by:

- *Thinking about the importance of involving school-age children in shaping program rules and limits.*

- *Exploring examples of things it's important to have rules about.*

- *Exploring guidelines for conducting rule-making sessions with school-age children and youth.*

- *Exploring consequences which can occur when rules are broken.*

- *Identifying strategies for helping children abide by program rules and take responsibility for their actions.*

Before moving on to the next section, use the techniques presented in **PART FIVE** as a resource for completing the sentences and answering the questions which follow. As you complete your answers, you may also find it helpful to review the information provided in **PART TWO, PART THREE, AND PART FOUR.** Review your answers with your supervisor or assigned mentor. Make changes and ask for help as needed.

- *Based on what I know about my school-age program and the school-age children who attend, I think the program rules and limits should focus on the following topics: (Include at least five topics you think are important - combine topics which are related)*

_____

_____

_____

_____

- *Select three of the topics you listed above and give an example of a rule that could be developed in relation to each topic. (Remember to be clear, simple, and positive.)*

_____

_____

_____

- *Read the following scenarios describing incidents where program rules are broken. Then use the space provided to answer the questions which follow each scenario.*

Scenario One: *Imagine your program has the following rules:*

1) Use program materials properly; if you don't know how, ask for help.

2) When you finish using toys or equipment, be sure to put them away.

Now think about the following incident: Tommy and Barrett, both eight-year-olds, are playing in the Board and Table Games Area. First they play Connect Four™, but the game quickly deteriorates when Tommy starts spinning the game pieces like tops.The pieces begin spinning off the table. Barrett starts laughing and joins in. When all the pieces are on the floor, the boys walk away and take the Mancala game off the shelf. They can't figure out how to play, so they begin shooting marbles across the floor; the marbles are flying everywhere.

1) How did Tommy and Barrett break the rules?

2) What might staff have done to prevent this situation?

3) What should happen because Tommy and Barrett broke the rules; what would be appropriate <u>consequences for their actions?</u>

4) How could similar situations be avoided in the future?

Scenario Two: *Imagine your program has the following rules:*

1) Show respect and use kind words.

2) If you have a problem, talk it out.

3) Treat program materials and equipment with respect.

Now think about the following incident: Seven-year-old Annika and six-year-old Shannon are playing in the dramatic play area. Shannon wants to play grocery store. Annika says she thinks it's boring to play grocery store. She wants to play beauty parlor. Shannon makes a face and sticks her tongue out at Annika and begins sorting out the plastic fruits and vegetables and displaying them on a shelf. Annika screams at her: "You are so stupid; I hate playing grocery and I'm going to wreck your store." Then she picks up the plastic food and begins throwing it all over the dramatic play area. Shannon retaliates by picking up curlers from the beauty parlor kit and throwing them at Annika.

1) How did Annika and Shannon break the rules?

2) What might staff have done to prevent this situation?

3) What should happen because Annika and Shannon broke the rules; what would be appropriate consequences of their actions?

4) How could similar situations be avoided in the future?

Note: You may want to compare your answers to the scenario questions with possible answers provided in the ***Answer Guide*** at the end of the book.

PART SIX:
Strategies for Planning Program Activities Children Will Enjoy

Planning Activities Which Are Linked to Developmental Needs and Interests.....

It is very likely you will be responsible for planning and leading activities in your school-age program. There are many resource books available which contain hundreds of ideas for school-age program activities. Your program may own some of them. You will also find many of them in your community library. Ask your program director to share planning resource books with you. Check **Appendix II** for a selected list of activity planning resources.

Whether you are responsible for activities which take place outdoors, in the gym, in the art area, in the science and nature area, or in some other location, it's very important to keep the children in mind while you do your planning. The tips below can help you select and plan successful activities:

Tips for Selecting and Planning Successful Program Activities[1]

1. How does the activity MATCH UP with the general needs and interests of children and youth in your program?

2. What is the PURPOSE of the activity? How will children and youth in your program BENEFIT from the activity?

3. Is the activity APPROPRIATE in view of what you know about the individual developmental needs and interests of children and youth in your program? If not, how could it be adapted or changed to make it more appropriate?

4. What additional EQUIPMENT, SUPPLIES, OR FURNITURE (if any) will be needed in the area where you will conduct the activity? Will you need to make any CHANGES to the area? Will you need to SET UP AHEAD OF TIME? Can children HELP set up?

5. How much TIME will it take to do the activity? Can additional time be provided for any children who become especially interested in the activity? Can the activity be EXTENDED AND EXPANDED OVER SEVERAL DAYS OR WEEKS if children want to continue working on it?

---

[1]Excerpted and adapted with permission from Roberta L. Newman, *Keys to Quality in School-Age Child Care* (1993). Union Bridge, MD: Summerwinds Communications.

6.   How much SUPERVISION will be needed for the activity? Will you need to REMAIN WITH THE ACTIVITY until all interested children are finished? Will it be SAFE for you to move to other program areas from time to time? What ROLE(S) will you play during the activity? Will you need HELP FROM A CO-WORKER while conducting the activity?

Ideas for Involving Children and Youth in Program Planning.....

When exploring the characteristic needs and interests of school-age children in **PART TWO,** you learned that as they grow and change they are moving toward independence and becoming very interested in planning and directing their own activities. This means it's very important for school-age staff to think of ways to involve them in program planning. By planning activities **WITH** children instead of **FOR** them, staff can help children develop a feeling of ownership of the program—a positive feeling that the program belongs to them.

Tips for Getting School-Agers Involved in Program Planning[2]

- *Talk informally and directly with children about things they like to do at home, at school, and in the program.* Ask them open-ended questions such as: "What's your favorite thing to do here? What could we do to make it better? What would you like to learn how to do?

- *Post a "Question of the Week" in a prominent place.* Select an open-ended question and post it in your Library, Writing, or other prominent area. Provide paper and pencils and an envelope for children to deposit their answers. Review the answers at the end of each week. Use the ideas to enrich program planning.

- *Help children build on what they are already doing.* (e.g. If children are working out a dance routine, ask how or if you can help. Do they need props or costumes? Special music? Do they want to organize a dance club? Invite a dancer to visit the program? Have a talent show?)

- *Set up a Suggestion Box.* Invite some of the children to help you design and decorate a suggestion box. Encourage children to use the box to share their ideas about ways to make the program more fun and interesting. Talk with children about how to incorporate their ideas.

- *Conduct an informal survey to find out about children's preferences.* Keep the questions short and simple. Consider inviting older children in the program to help conduct a poll, interview others, and tabulate and report on the responses. Ask questions such as: What is your favorite thing to do in the program? What is your least favorite thing to do in our program? If you could add one thing to the program, what would it be? If you were in charge of our program for one day, what changes would you make?

---

[2]Excerpted and adapted with permission from Roberta L. Newman, *Planning Program Activities, Schedules, and Staff Roles* (1998). Cape Charles, VA: Cape Charles Development Company.

- *Start a Program Leadership Club.* Invite interested children to meet regularly (at least once a week) with you to discuss ideas for improving the program. Use the time for the following activities: brainstorm activity ideas, identify places to visit or people to invite to the program, plan clubs, solve problems in the program, brainstorm food items for snack, plan special program events or festivals. Help children evaluate their ideas to determine which ones are workable and which ones are not. Explore alternatives if the first ideas children come up with aren't feasible.

- *Invite children to help design, decorate, set up, and re-arrange areas of the program environment.* School-age children have many good ideas about how to organize, decorate, and arrange the areas they use for work and play. Invite them to help create the environment.

Making the Most of Your Program Environment.....

School-age programs take place in many different kinds of facilities. Regardless of where your program is housed, it's important for you to assume responsibility for creating and maintaining a safe, pleasant program environment.

- Ensure that materials and supplies are well-maintained.

- Check your area for safety and health hazards every day. Report any concerns to your supervisor.

- Arrange your area to make it inviting, attractive, accessible, and functional for the children.

- If you share space, take a creative, problem-solving approach to sharing the space with others:

     1) Invite children to help with daily set-up and take-down.

     2) Keep key players who share your space informed about your program activities and needs (e.g. custodians, school principals, teachers, and others). Invite them to visit. Express appreciation for their cooperation.

     3) Fulfill your obligations and responsibilities for maintaining and caring for shared space.

Other Tips for Program Planning.....

Your experience as a school-age staff member will be very rewarding if you find ways to work with others to plan, implement, and enhance your ideas for program activities. Here are some suggestions:

- Exchange ideas with co-workers so that you can function as a team as you plan program activities.

- Identify THEMES which interest the children and work with children and co-workers to plan activities which relate to these themes. (See Appendix II for resources on theme-based programming.)

- Plan a variety of simultaneous activities to provide children with choices throughout the program day.

- Be prepared with "back pocket" activities for use during transition times (arrival, dismissal, moving to another program area) and at times when plans must be adjusted due to a program "emergency" (e.g. the field trip bus breaks down, special guest performer is late and the kids are already gathered for the performance, a child's parents have been delayed, etc.). See Appendix II on pages 61-62 for examples of "back pocket activities" - activities that can be done "off the cuff" without advance preparation or props.
  (**TIP:** Share the games with your co-workers. Learn the ones you like best. Copy the directions and carry them with you so you're always ready to play!)

Tips for Leading Games and Involving Children in Group Activities.....

Staff who are successful at leading group games and activities take time to learn the directions and how to play any game or activity they want to lead. They try out the game with co-workers, friends, or family. This helps build confidence as a game leader. They also think about how they will ***introduce and teach*** the activity or game to children; they take a systematic approach. In his book, *How to Play with Kids*, nationally recognized Play Leader Jim Therrell offers a variety of tips and techniques for being an effective leader of games and activities. Below is a list of key principles from his book.[3]

- *Use the step by step DDADA technique when introducing a new game:*
  Describe the game
  Demonstrate how to do it
  Ask if there are any questions
  Do it
  Adapt it (Make it easier, more challenging, or change it in some other way, as needed)

- *Use developmental awareness. Choose games carefully based on the needs, abilities, skills, and interests of children and youth in your program.*

- *Use playful "attention getters" to get things started. (e.g. a creative sound, movement, a pre-taught ritual or collaborative game activity.)*

---

[3] Excerpted and adapted with permission from Jim Therrell, *How to Play with Kids* (1992) Austin, TX: Play Today Press.

- *Maintain eye contact for active listening.*

- *Always be energetic and enthusiastic when introducing and playing games.*

- *Help kids develop safety consciousness by setting appropriate physical and psychological boundaries and limits* (e.g. agree on how and where you may touch people in a game of tag, talk about avoiding taunting or teasing)

- *Develop a MAXIMUM ACTIVITY PLAN (MAP). A* **MAP** is a plan for greater participation per person. Choose games carefully based on the kids involved, the situation, the time of day, etc. Use smaller groups when possible. Institute rule innovations to increase participation; try to develop rules where no one will be eliminated, rather than rules where more and more kids are out. The more kids who are "out" on the sidelines, the greater the chance behavior problems will develop as they look for something to do while waiting. (e.g. Instead of traditional "Musical Chairs" where one person at a time is out when no chair is available, play "Cooperative Musical Chairs" where children share chairs as more and more chairs are removed. The game ends when everyone tries to share the last chair.)

- *Set goals for playing games.* It usually takes a good plan to insure that games are fun, playful, and interesting for children. When planning, write down your goals, know exactly WHY you are introducing activities, and communicate your thinking clearly to children.

WHAT I'VE LEARNED ABOUT PLANNING AND LEADING PROGRAM ACTIVITIES CHILDREN WILL ENJOY

In **PART SIX,** you have explored various strategies for conducting successful activities by:

- *Linking activities to developmental needs and interests.*
- *Learning about techniques for involving children and youth in program planning.*
- *Making the most of the program environment.*
- *Sharing ideas and making plans with co-workers.*
- *Exploring "back pocket" activity ideas and how to use them.*
- *Thinking about how to introduce and lead games and activities effectively.*

Before moving on to the next section, take a few minutes to think about how to use this information in your work with school-age children and youth. On a sheet of paper write down your ideas for planning and leading successful activities. As you complete this section, you may also find it helpful to review information provided in **PARTS TWO, THREE, FOUR, AND FIVE.** When you've finished, review your ideas with your supervisor and make any needed changes. You may want to compare your ideas for the two scenarios with the possible answers provided in the **Answer Key** at the end of the book.

- *Think about the following scenario and write down some ideas for planning activities which would interest the children in the scenario. Include ideas for involving them in the planning process.*

Scenario One. Lately many kids in your program have taken an interest in stringing beads. Several five- and six-year-old boys string large beads on heavy cord to make bracelets for their moms. Some find it easy, others are having a hard time tying a knot in the cord to get started. Their beads often fall off and go rolling onto the floor. Sometimes they pick them up; sometimes they don't. A number of eight-, nine-, and ten-year-old girls and boys also use all kinds of beads to make bracelets, necklaces, rings, sandals to wear barefoot, and jewelry for the dolls in the dramatic play corner. Some of them are very skilled; others are having difficulty. But everywhere you look, you see kids stringing beads; they carry their projects with them, even to the gym and outdoors. Some of the kids sit and string beads while they watch others play board games. They can't seem to find a comfortable area to do their beading; as a result, you're finding beads everywhere.

1. What could you do to support and build on the children's interests in stringing beads?

2. How could you help them increase their skills?

- *Think about the following scenario and select a "back pocket" game or activity that you think would be appropriate in this situation. Give reasons for your selection.*

Scenario Two. You, two other co-workers, and 30 children from your program have been spending the day on a field trip to the zoo. After several hours walking around the zoo, you have gathered in a grassy spot next to the zoo entrance to wait for the bus to take you back to the center. The bus is late. Children are hot and tired. They begin to complain that they are bored. Several children begin chasing each other. You are near a crowded street and are afraid the children may run into the street. You know you need to pull the group together and help them calm down.

*In this situation, I would choose the following "Back Pocket" activity:_____
My reasons for choosing this activity are:*

- *Review the ideas for involving school-age children and youth in program planning. Choose one of the ideas which you would like to try out in your program. Write down your ideas here.*

- *Think about the area where you will work in your program. Then answer the following questions:*
    1) What ideas do you have for making the area pleasant, inviting, and attractive to school-age children and youth? Who else will be working with you in the area and how can you work together to make the most of the area?

    2) What responsibilities will you have for maintaining, displaying, and replenishing materials used in the area? What tasks will be involved? How will you get organized?

PART SEVEN:
Handling Problems and Conflicts Among School-Age Children

Setting a Positive Tone from the Beginning.....

Whenever there are two or more people in the same place, there is a potential for disagreement and conflict. Conflict is a natural part of being alive. Even though we may want to avoid it, conflict often provides us with challenges which help us grow, use creativity, exercise self-control, and learn how to solve problems. However, we also want to do as much as possible to avoid and prevent unnecessary conflicts. As a school-age staff member, you can do a lot to prevent unnecessary conflicts:

- *Talk with children in advance to share ideas for how they can work together in a positive way. PART THREE* offers suggestions for setting a positive tone with children on your first day. You may want to review these ideas.

- *Recognize that children have varying abilities and skills for handling problems and conflicts. PART TWO* discusses some of the differences among children. By keeping these differences in mind, you will be able to guide children in a way which reduces the possibility of conflict.

- *Keep in mind the DO's and DON'Ts identified by school-age directors in PART FOUR of this book.* Many conflicts arise when staff fail to keep these guidelines in mind.

- *Work with children to establish program rules and limits everyone agrees to live by. PART FIVE* contains many ideas for developing effective rules and guidelines.

- *Plan activities which are linked to children's developmental needs and are appropriate for your program setting. PART SIX* outlines techniques for planning successful activities which will help children work together in a spirit of cooperation.

Teaching Children Step-by-Step Problem Solving Strategies.....

There are a number of good books which contain lots of good ideas for helping children learn how to avoid conflicts and practice problem solving skills. Several of them are listed in *Appendix II.* They provide helpful, creative ideas for teaching problem solving through cooperative games, role playing, peace tables, clubs, and group discussion. Use them as a resource as you continue your work with school-age children.

As you begin your work, use the steps presented in the box below to teach children how to solve problems one step at a time. This will help them develop ownership of their problems and assume a sense of responsibility for their actions. It will also help them identify and express their emotions, opinions, and concerns appropriately.

Steps for Effective Problem Solving:

1) *STOP and CALM DOWN.* Do whatever it takes to get yourself feeling neutral. Take a few deep breaths. Relax; count to 10. Get a drink of water. Remove yourself from the group and close your eyes for a minute. *Remember, no one can use thinking skills to solve a problem or conflict when they are feeling angry, upset, or hurt.*

2) *GET TOGETHER TO FIGURE OUT THE CAUSE OF THE PROBLEM. WHAT IS THE PROBLEM ABOUT?* You may want to take turns describing the problem and sharing your feelings, wants, and opinions related to the problem. Listen without interrupting. Don't talk about *solutions* until you agree on *what the problem is about*.

3) *BRAINSTORM IDEAS FOR SOLVING THE PROBLEM.* Make a list of all the possible solutions - practical and impractical. Don't judge yet.

4) *EVALUATE THE IDEAS FOR SOLVING THE PROBLEM.* Choose the best idea(s) and use them to *PLAN* a course of action.

5) *PUT YOUR PLAN INTO ACTION.* Decide on a time and place to check your progress - how is your plan working? Do you need to do anything else?

Learning to Recognize the Common Causes of Conflicts in School-Age Programs.....

There are certain problems which occur often in school-age programs. The contents of this book are designed to help you anticipate and avoid many of them. The checklist in the box on the next page can help you identify what might be causing conflicts which arise in your program. Then use a step-by-step problem solving process to correct the situation.

**Checklist of Common Causes of Conflicts in School-Age Programs**[4]

**Use this Checklist to Identify Possible Causes of Conflicts in Your Program**

_____ **Inappropriate or poorly planned program activities.**

_____ **Inappropriate use or lack of suitable space, equipment, or supplies.**

_____ **Poor handling of transition times - too much waiting between activities.**

_____ **Failure to spot or anticipate problems about to happen.**

_____ **Lack of understanding of children's needs, resulting in a mismatch between the children's capabilities and the expectations of the program.**

_____ **Personality or temperament clashes among children or between staff and children.**

_____ **Overly competitive atmosphere.**

_____ **Intolerant/unfriendly atmosphere.**

_____ **Poor communication (by children and/or adults who can't or don't express needs appropriately, can't observe, don't know how or refuse to listen).**

_____ **Misuse of power by staff - expectations too high, too authoritarian or controlling**

_____ **Too many or unreasonable rules - failure to involve children in shaping rules.**

_____ **Absence of problem-solving skills.**

_____ **Lack of clarity about what the expectations are, how things are organized, what the limits and boundaries are.**

Tips for Diffusing and Reducing Conflicts When They Emerge.....

It is unrealistic to think that you will be able to eliminate all conflicts in your program. In addition to step-by-step problem solving, the techniques listed in the box on the next page may be helpful when conflicts begin to emerge. It's important to remember that **no technique** will work in every situation. You will need to use good judgment in deciding what techniques will work best depending on who is involved, your own capabilities, the cause(s) of the conflict, and the setting.

---

[4] Excerpted and adapted with permission from Roberta L. Newman, _Keys to Quality in School-Age Child Care_ (1993) Union Bridge, MD: Summerwinds Communications.

Techniques Staff Can Use to Diffuse or Reduce Conflict Situations

- *Get your own feelings under control.* Act with firmness and authority if needed. But never vent your anger with children.

- *Ignore the behavior.* Assume it won't get worse and don't fuel it with your attention.

- *Intervene immediately if children are in danger of hurting each other.* Help them find ways to use words to talk through their issues.

- *Redirect children.* Help children get involved in a different activity. Invite them to help you with a chore. Help them start a new game.

- *Help children withdraw temporarily if they are out of control.* Help them think of ways to cool off and "get themselves together." This is especially helpful when children are very angry, crying, or having a temper tantrum.

- *Use special signals.* Use eye contact or gestures to alert a child of the need for self control. This is most effective if you and a child have agreed on the special signal in advance.

- *Move closely to children when you see signs they may be losing control.*

- *Show interest.* If children look bored, sad, upset, angry, engage the child in conversation. Let them know you are interested in their problems, concerns, fears, ideas, etc.

- *Use humor.* Make a joke to ease the tension. Be sure to use humor with sensitivity. Never use humor to make fun of children.

- *Give assistance.* Offer help and support when children might not understand directions or feel frustrated.

- *Change the routine.* Break the tension with a change of pace if an inappropriate activity or schedule seems to be causing the problem.

- *Remove objects which cause problems.* Put away or move objects which seem to bring out negative behavior and provoke conflicts.

Becoming Aware of Your Conflict Management Style.....

Most of us have developed a style for dealing with conflicts in our lives:

- Some routinely *ignore* conflicts.

- Some always try to *accommodate* other people and smooth things over if at all possible. If we do this too often, we often find we are giving up on things we really care about.

- Some tend to *look for compromises*, taking the attitude that if you give up something, I will too. An over emphasis on compromising can mean that no one ever wins - instead we all lose a little.

- Some want to work things out so that everybody wins all the time. We spend a lot of time trying to *collaborate* as a way of resolving conflicts. With collaboration, everybody wins, but it may take a lot of time to get to the solution.

- Some take a hard line position. When they're right, they're right. They maintain a position of *authority and control* no matter what!

Take a minute to think about your own style of managing conflicts. Do you use one style much more than others? Do you vary between one or two styles? Do you use some styles a lot and others not at all? People who specialize in conflict management have learned that *no conflict management style is appropriate for every situation. It all depends on who's involved, how people are feeling, and what is happening in the situation.*

As you work with school-age children, try to become aware of your own style of responding to conflicts when they arise. If you think you would like to know more about conflict management and how to develop the skills to use different styles, consult the following resources listed in *Appendix II: Creative Conflict Resolution* and *Adventures in Peacemaking.*

Asking for Help with Difficult Problems and Conflicts

Used consistently and appropriately, the suggestions and techniques in this book will help you provide positive guidance and resolve problems and conflicts effectively in most situations. However, you may find that there are situations which you are not able to handle effectively. Or you may feel you do not know how to respond effectively to children who exhibit challenging behavior or intense anger. *Be sure to ask your supervisor for help when you are feeling this way.* You may be able to participate in additional training in how to handle difficult situations. Or your supervisor may feel it's appropriate to contact resource people in the community to provide support for a child or family experiencing extreme difficulties.

WHAT I'VE LEARNED ABOUT HANDLING PROBLEMS AND CONFLICTS AMONG SCHOOL-AGE CHILDREN AND YOUTH

In **PART SEVEN,** you have learned about different ways to manage problems and conflicts in your school-age program by:

- *Thinking about how to set a positive tone with children from the beginning.*
- *Learning about step-by-step problem solving strategies.*
- *Learning to recognize common causes of conflicts in school-age programs.*
- *Exploring tips for diffusing and reducing conflicts when they emerge.*
- *Identifying different conflict management styles.*
- *Reflecting on my own style of managing conflicts.*
- *Thinking about the importance of asking for help with difficult situations.*

Before moving on to the next section, apply your knowledge to the scenario below. When you've finished, review your ideas with your supervisor and make any needed changes. You may want to compare your ideas with possible answers provided in the **Answer Key** at the end of the book.

- ***Think about the following scenario and respond to the questions that follow:***

Scenario. *Every day a number of eight-year-old children rush to the game area as soon as they arrive. They want to get to the Connect Four™ game before anyone else gets there. The children are in such a rush to be first that they sometimes neglect to put their book bags in their cubbies. They throw them on the floor. Two of the children always seem to get there first; they push other kids out of the way who may be in their path. Today, a child fell and bumped his head on a shelf as a result of being shoved by one of the Connect Four™ kids. Things are out of control. The kids who don't get there first are frustrated and angry, and begin shouting: "You always get to play Connect Four™. We want it today." The children who got there first, say "No way. We got here first."*

1. What do you think might be the cause(s) behind this conflict situation?

2. What techniques could staff have used early on to diffuse, reduce, or prevent the conflict?

3. How could staff apply step-by-step problem solving to help children resolve the conflict?

PART EIGHT:
Connecting with Parents and Families in School-Age Programs

Helping Parents Feel Welcome, Accepted, and Valued.....

Even though they are beginning to explore and interact with the world beyond home and family, children and youth still view parents as central to their lives. They look to them for help in interpreting and understanding their experiences in a changing world. Because parents and families are so important to the children and youth in your program, it's essential for you to do everything you can to help parents feel welcome, valued, and appreciated. Listed below are examples of things you can do every day to create a "family friendly" atmosphere.

Ideas for Reaching Out to Parents as Partners with School-Age Programs[5]

- *Learn parents' names; smile and greet them by name whenever you see them.*

- *Show interest in parents.* Ask them about their day or their weekend, extend a compliment, inquire about a special family event their child has mentioned to you - arrival of a baby, a new pet, a visit from grandma, a recent trip or celebration.

- *Remember interesting, funny, or clever things children say and do during the program; take a moment to share these stories with parents when you see them.*

- *Consider setting up a "parent comfort corner" where parents can relax, fill out a field trip form, or chat with another parent.* If space allows, provide a small table, a couple of comfortable chairs, a basket of magazines related to parenting and families. You might even set up a coffee pot with hot water and a basket of supplies for coffee and tea. Provide a jar for donations if needed.

- *Take pictures of children involved in program activities and share them with parents. Use a video camera if available and loan the tape to parents so they can get a close look at what the program is like.*

- *Encourage parents to participate in program activities.* (e.g. field trips, clubs, sharing knowledge or skills related to their interests and occupations)

- *Invite parents to share family traditions by coming in to cook family recipes, sending in photos of family celebrations or trips, helping plan a special program event related to their cultural traditions.*

- *Set up a Parent Bulletin Board for sharing important information and news about the program.* Keep parents well informed in advance about any policy or procedural changes which will affect them.

---

[5] Excerpted and adapted with permission from Roberta L. Newman, *Building Relationships with Parents and Families* (1998) Nashville, TN: School-Age NOTES.

- ***Help parents get to know you.*** Let them know about your interests, hobbies, educational background and experiences with school-age children. Wear a name tag to help parents identify you during the first few weeks of the program.

- ***Play the role of social director.*** Introduce parents to each other. They have much in common.

- ***Treat parents with respect; be empathetic about stresses they may be experiencing.*** Talk with your supervisor about how to handle difficult situations involving parents.

WHAT I'VE LEARNED ABOUT CONNECTING WITH PARENTS AND FAMILIES IN SCHOOL-AGE PROGRAMS

In **PART EIGHT,** you have thought about ways to help parents feel welcome, accepted, and valued by:

- *Exploring the important role parents play in the lives of children and youth.*
- *Exploring ways to reach out to parents as partners with your school-age program.*

Before moving on to the next section, think about the following questions and record your answers in the space provided. Share your answers with your supervisor. Add ideas and make adjustments as needed.

- *Based on what you know about your program, the children and youth you will serve, and your job responsibilities, what are some things you can do to be sure you have positive interactions with parents and families?*

- *What concerns or questions do you have about how to have positive interactions with parents in your program?*

- *What is the most important thing you want to keep in mind when interacting with parents in your program?*

WRAPPING UP:
KEYS TO SUCCESS AS A SCHOOL-AGE STAFF MEMBER

Using Diverse Roles as a School-Age Staff Member.....

Staff in quality programs play many different roles. Listed below are some examples of important roles school-age staff play[6]:

- *Activity Leader.* You play the role of **Activity Leader** when you introduce a new game in the gym or outdoors, involve children in a group art project, or conduct a science experiment.

- *Facilitator.* You play the role of **Facilitator** when you help children make choices about what to do, help them find resources to support their activities, or help them redirect their activities in a positive direction.

- *Teacher.* You play the role of **Teacher** when you teach children a song, a dance step, how to use a microscope, how to serve a volleyball, how to weave, how to use new software, or other new skills, methods, or techniques.

- *Participant.* You are a **Participant** when you play a board game with children, join them for a game of kickball, do an act in their talent show, learn magic tricks with them, or add your artistic expression to a group mural.

- *Problem Solver.* You play the role of **Problem Solver** when you help children figure out what's wrong with a piece of equipment and how to fix it, think of ways to share gym space for a variety of physical sports and games, find a way to save and display their ongoing projects, or develop a plan for sharing materials and equipment.

- *Mediator.* You play the role of **Mediator** when you help children talk through their problems before someone gets hurt, help children talk to each other about their feelings, or help children make amends when they have damaged another child's project or personal property.

- *Observer.* You play the role of **Observer** when you <u>pay close attention</u> to what children are saying and doing and use your observations to plan program activities and experiences which match their needs and interests.

- *Listener.* You play the role of **Listener** when you spend time learning about what children like to do, what they care about, and how they are feeling about themselves and others.

---

[6] Excerpted and adapted with permission from Roberta L. Newman, *Keys to Quality in School-Age Child Care* (1993) Union Bridge, MD: Summerwinds Communications.

- *Coach.* You play the role of **Coach** in any area of your program when you help children work together as a team, assess their readiness to learn new skills, provide them with just the right amount of challenge and opportunity, and encourage them to keep trying until they succeed.

- *Collaborator.* You play the role of **Collaborator** when you join with children to form a special club, build a fort on the playground, or work with children to plan and carry out a talent show, game day, or celebration.

- *Role Model.* You act as a **Role Model** when you handle problems calmly; communicate politely; demonstrate good sportsmanship and teamwork; extend friendship and kindness to everyone; exhibit patience and care when learning how to do something new; treat program materials, equipment, and facilities with care.

As you work with school-age children each day, look for opportunities to play many different roles. The more roles you are able to play effectively, the better you will be at working with children with different needs, abilities, and interests. Playing a variety of roles makes your work more satisfying and exciting because it helps you discover different ways to support, encourage, and inspire children to be the best they can be. Playing different roles can be challenging, but it's well worth the effort!

Tips for Success During the First Few Months......

During your first days, weeks, and months working with school-age children, you may have many questions about your new responsibilities. You may even become confused about policies and procedures or about how to handle a difficult situation. This is to be expected because *THERE IS A LOT TO LEARN!* Here are a few tips which can help you move through the few months with success and build your confidence as a school-age professional:

- *Recognize there is a lot to learn.* Don't make assumptions until you know the facts.

- *Ask lots of questions.* When you don't know what to do, go to your supervisor or to a mentor who has been assigned to help you

- *Exercise resourcefulness.* Review program policies and support systems designed to help you and make use of them. Make the most of resources around you—co-workers, activity books, tapes and training videos, workshops related to school-age care. Explore program materials and equipment and learn how to use them.

- *Face issues directly; communicate politely and openly.* Avoid gossip. Avoid making assumptions about the intentions and motives of others. Look for guidance and information from reliable sources.

- *Use the topics you have explored in this book as a foundation for building your knowledge and skills as a school-age staff member.* Consult them often as a resource.

They provide important keys to developing a satisfying and successful work experience in school-age programs. Here is a reminder list of the major topics you explored in the previous sections:

✓ You looked at the history of the school-age field, how it is growing, what it takes to be effective as a staff member, and how your own interests and skills match with the emerging profession of school-age care.

✓ You explored the characteristics and developmental needs of school-age children and thought about ways to support them in school-age programs.

✓ You learned strategies, tips, and techniques for getting off to a good start on your first day of work.

✓ You explored common DO's and DON'Ts for staff in school-age programs.

✓ You learned strategies for developing and implementing program rules and guidelines.

✓ You learned strategies for planning program activities children will enjoy.

✓ You explored ideas for handling problems and conflicts among school-agers.

✓ You explored ways to connect with parents in school-age programs.

NOTES

APPENDIX I:

ANSWER GUIDE

PART TWO

Scenario One

Developmental tasks the different boys are working on:
* They are using small muscles to develop fine motor skills.
* Kyle is using new thinking skills to organize and plan his activities. He is also working on becoming more independent and competent.
* Mario and Tommy are using new thinking skills to plan, experiment, and design their city; using imaginations to think about what it would be like to live in their city; using their increasing attention spans to expand their project to the next day. They are exploring the world beyond home and family as they discuss earthquakes and the news.

Ways you could support, help, guide, or encourage each child:
* You provide Kyle with different size Legos which might be easier to manipulate on his own.
* You could place a "Save Please" sign next to the city so they can work on it the next day. If that isn't possible, you could take a picture of the city so they could remember how it was built or help them make a diagram to use as a guide for rebuilding.

Scenario Two

Developmental tasks Haley and Jasmine are working on:
* They are using new thinking skills to imagine what they will do when they grow up.
* They are interested in becoming competent.
* They are exploring the world beyond home and family as they think about the field of fashion design.
* They are working on independence as they use their resourcefulness as they gather supplies.
* They are using creative expression to express new thoughts and feelings.

Ways you could support, help, guide, or encourage them:
* Provide a wider variety of art materials to encourage creativity.
* Encourage them to make a collage of fashion designs, using photos from selected magazines.
* Provide books on fashion design and designers, drawing human figures.
* Provide sewing activities and teach sewing skills.
* Help them plan and carry out a fashion show.

Scenario Three

Developmental tasks Maria and Belinda are working on:
* They are working on becoming more competent and independent.
* They are expanding their worlds beyond home and family as they learn about arts and crafts from other countries.
* They are developing fine motor skills through craft activities.

Ideas for helping Maria make the most of her interests, abilities, talents, and family background:
* Arrange for her to teach crafts to other children.
* Display her work in the art area; help her set up an exhibit.
* Provide her with additional books and materials for expanding on her interests in crafts.
* Invite her grandmother to visit the program and share pictures and artifacts from her travels.

Scenario Four

Ideas you have for helping, supporting, and guiding children:
* Change the location of the game - move it away from the small hill.
* Adjust the equipment to make it easier to play - e.g. remove the net and lay a rope on the ground to mark the center line.
* Adapt the techniques used - e.g. have children toss the ball, rather than serve it. Or suggest they roll the ball back and forth.

Scenario Five

Temperamental characteristics which could be related to Kendra's behavior:
* Tendency to shy away from new experiences
* Tendency to act without thinking and respond to others intensely.

Ideas for helping her get involved in the rope-jumping activity:
* Ask Kendra if she would like to jump rope with you. Invite another child to join you.
* Ask her if she would like to join the group already jumping. If she says yes, talk to her about how she could let them know.

Scenario Six

Temperamental characteristics which could be related to Sammy's behavior:
* Tendency to be distractible, to act without thinking.
* Short attention span.
* High activity level.

Changes staff could make to help Sammy connect with the program.
* Help him focus by greeting him when he comes in the door and reminding him to hang up his belongings.
* Position yourself nearby during group meetings.
* Give him an opportunity to exercise and blow off steam as soon as possible.

PART FIVE

Scenario One

How Tommy and Barrett broke the rules:
* They didn't use materials properly.
* They didn't ask for help when they didn't know how to play the game.
* They didn't put the game away when they were finished.

What staff might have done to prevent this situation:
* Monitor the area closely to help children make good choices about what materials to use.
* Make regular offers to teach children how to play games.
* Post a sign in the area reminding children to ask for help when they need it.

What should happen - what would be appropriate consequences:
* Point out they haven't treated the games properly. Remind them how important it is to take care of games and other equipment so they will last.
* Require them to work together to pick up the game pieces and store them away properly.
* Tell them they may remain in the area if they think they can treat the games properly. Offer to help them learn how to use the games properly. Offer to teach them the game rules and procedures. Or ask a child to help them who knows how to play.

How similar situations could be avoided in the future:
* Post a sign in the area reminding children to ask for help when they need it.
* Invite children who are good at games to take on the responsibility of teaching others how to play.
* Provide close supervision of the game area.
* Be sure all games are in good condition and displayed neatly.
* Give children who are ready for responsibilities the opportunity to help maintain the game area.

Scenario Two

How Annika and Shannon broke the rules:
* They were disrespectful of each other and used unkind words.
* They failed to treat program materials and equipment with respect.
* They tried to solve their problem physically rather than talking it out.

What staff might have done to prevent the situation:
* Help the girls find a way to divide the area so both activities can take place.

What should happen - what would be appropriate consequences:
* Help the girls calm down and use problem solving skills to talk about what happened.
* Remind them of the rules and require the girls to pick up the props and put them away.
* Tell the girls they may remain in the area if they will treat each other kindly and take proper care of the materials. If they agree, allow them to stay. If they are not ready to agree, require them to leave the area for awhile.

How similar situations could be avoided in the future:
* Look at how the dramatic play area is set up; make changes if there is not enough room for children's activities. Be sure there are enough props, but not too many for the space available.
* Join children during dramatic play activities and act as a role model of kind, respectful behavior.
* Monitor the dramatic play area closely and intervene before situations escalate.

PART SEVEN

Scenario - Connect Four™ Conflict

Possible causes behind this situation:
* There is only one Connect Four™ game.
* There are not enough alternative games to choose from.
* Some of the children involved have temperamental traits which lead them to be intense and to act without thinking.
* Children do not know how to use problem-solving skills.

Techniques staff could have used early on to diffuse, reduce, or prevent the conflict:
* Remove the Connect Four™ game temporarily; then hold a meeting to discuss the situation.

How staff could apply step-by-step problem solving to help children resolve the conflict:
* Gather the group; point out they are out of control. Give suggestions to help them collect themselves (some deep breaths, count to 10, etc.)
* Ask each child to talk about the problem from his or her point of view. Make a list of possible causes.
* Brainstorm ideas for solving the problem - buy more games? Ask for donations of games? Make home-made games? Have a sign-up sheet for games we have? What else?
* Choose the best solution(s) and make a plan for working on the solution(s).
* Meet again soon to talk about how it's going.

Management style which would be most effective in this situation:
* Collaborating would work the best because it gets everyone involved in owning and solving the problem.

APPENDIX II:

Back Pocket Activities - NO PROP Games and Activities to Use on the Spot!

Observation Game. Announce it's time for observation. Walk around asking certain children to stand while others remain seated. The object is to have someone in the group discover the reason why some children are standing while others remain seated. What do the children have in common who are standing up? *Example* - children wearing blue, girls wearing ribbons, children with glasses, children with high top tennis shoes.

That's Good. What kind of bad things can you think of to say about something you really like? Think of something that everyone likes or thinks of as nice. Now try to describe this thing to your friends without telling them what it is and say ONLY BAD THINGS. Try to make this thing sound as awful as you can without saying anything untrue or anything that makes it easy to guess. *Example* - You love bubble gum. But you describe it by saying: It gets very sticky when wet. If you get it in your hair, you may have to cut your hair off. If you step on it, you might not be able to move.

The Magic Box. Gather the group in a circle. Tell them there is an invisible "Magic Box" sitting in the middle of the circle. Go over to the box and pretend to take something out of the box. Then act out what it is. It might be a telephone, a ball, a hula hoop, even an elephant! Use actions which help children guess what it is. The child who guesses correctly takes the next turn.

Decorate the Room with the Closed Door. Set aside a large space in the middle of the room or outdoor area. Begin the activity by telling the group they will be decorating an invisible room with a closed door. Walk around the area to show the children where the walls of the room are located. Indicate that a door is located on one of the walls and demonstrate how the door opens and closes. Ask the group what kind of room they would like to decorate - kitchen, bedroom, family room, dining room? Then, have each child pantomime carrying an object or piece of furniture into the room. Everyone must remember to open and shut the door as they enter and exit to make their delivery. When everyone has placed something in the room, have group members try to describe everything the room contains. This is a great game to test your memory - it works well with older kids.

Quick Change Model. Invite one child to come up in front of the group. Ask the child to turn around three times slowly while the rest of the children are looking at how he is dressed. They might notice his shirt is tucked in, shoes are tied, socks are up, he is wearing a belt or watch. The child then leaves the area and quickly changes something. When the child returns, the children try to guess what has changed. Did he remove the watch? roll up his socks? pull out his shirt? *Variations on this game: 1) have the child change 2 or 3 items, or 2) have children work in pairs - children face each other to observe what the other person is wearing, then turn back to back and change something, then face again and try to guess the change(s).*

Good Morning, Judge. One child sits down with his back to the rest of the group. One at a time the leader (you or one of the kids) points to a child in the group. The child must say *"Good Morning, Judge."* and disguise his or her voice. The child with his back to the group can ask for one repeat per speaker and then has to take a guess as to who is speaking. If the child guesses correctly, another child is selected to say *"Good Morning, Judge."* Three incorrect guesses mean it's time to let someone else have a turn being the guesser.

More "Back Pocket" Activities - What to Do When There's Nothing to Do!

Giants, Wizards, Elves. Tell children there is a kingdom with three types of beings: *Giants* stand on their toes and stretch very high. *Wizards* wave their hands forward as if sending out a spell. *Elves* squat down and look very tiny. *Giants* easily overpower the *Elves*. But *Giants* are always outsmarted by the *Wizards*. *Elves* are very clever and confuse the *Wizards*. With this background, divide the group into two teams. Agree on a center line to separate the teams and two back goal lines. Each team huddles behind their goal line to decide whether team members will be *Giants, Wizards, or Elves*. Once they have made their decisions, the teams approach the center line and at the count of three chant: *Giants, Wizards, Elves*. Immediately they act out their team identity. If *Elves* end up facing *Giants*, the *Giants* can capture them by tagging them as they run for safety behind their goal line. If *Elves* face *Wizards*, the *Elves* try to do the capturing. If *Wizards* face *Giants*, the *Wizards* try to do the capturing. Any player caught before they reach their goal line becomes a member of the other team. Teams rehuddle and choose their next identity. The game continues until one team has been totally captured by the other team.

Shark and Tuna. All but two players circle and hold hands. One free player is a *Shark*, the other is a *Tuna*. *Shark* tries to capture *Tuna*. When *Tuna* runs through the circle, children raise their arms to let him through, but when *Shark* tries to get through, they lower them. Game continues until *Tuna* is caught.

Octopus. In a defined area one child is designated the *Octopus*. *Octopus* runs after the other players and attempts to tag them. When *Octopus* tags a player, the player is frozen, but can wave his or her arms like the tentacles of an *Octopus*, helping tag others until all are *Octopi*.

Field Trip Fantasy. Have children work in groups of 4 or 5 and ask them to come up with a list of 10 things they would take with them if they were going on a *Sea Cruise, a River Boat Ride, A Desert Camp Out, a Trip to the Moon, a Hike through a Rain Forest,* or another fantastic place. Gather the group and have them share their answers, giving reasons for what they decided to bring along.

The Play's the Thing. Have children work with a few friends and make up a skit using characters from a favorite book, TV show, movie, etc. Have them perform their skit for the others. *(You may need to remind children to use appropriate language and appropriate touching.)*

Spin a Yarn. Sit in a circle and give one child a ball of yarn. The child with the yarn makes up a sentence or thought to start a story (*e.g. "When Joey woke up, he saw a bright green light outside the window."*) The child passes the yarn to the next child who adds another sentence which builds on the first child's idea. The game continues until everyone has had a turn to help *"spin the yarn."* Tip: encourage the children to keep the yarn going to the end rather than ending it by having the characters run away or disappear before everyone has a chance. If you come up with a great yarn, build on it and create a skit. OR act it out in slow motion or in silence.

The Red Hat. Gather children in a circle. Place an imaginary *"Red Hat"* in the middle of the circle. Tell the children the hat has special powers - when you put it on, you can become anything or anybody you want to be - a certain movie star, an athlete, an airline pilot, a mother with a baby, a gas station attendant, a bus tour guide, etc. Encourage children to pick roles and occupations that take imagination to demonstrate and might be hard to guess. *Variation: Have children work in pairs. One child takes on a secret identity; the other child conducts an interview and tries to guess the friend's identity. The identity might be a person, a machine, an appliance, a toy, etc.*

APPENDIX III:

Basic Resources You Can Use Now:

Fink, Dale Borman. *Discipline in School-Age Care: Control the Climate, Not the Children.* 1995. Nashville: School-Age NOTES.

Haas-Foletta, Karen and Michele Cogley. *School-Age Ideas and Activities for After-School Programs.* 1990. Nashville: School-Age NOTES.

Kasser, Susan L. *Inclusive Games: Movement Fun for Everyone!* 1995. Champaign: Human Kinetics.

Michaelis, Bill and John M. O'Connell. *The Game and Play Leader's Handbook: Facilitating Fun and Positive Interaction.* 2000. State College: Venture Publishing.

Michaelis, Bill. *How to Lead Games.* (Video). 1997. Fremont: Radworks.

Moore, Annette C. *The Game Finder: A Leader's Guide to Great Activities.* 1992. State College: Venture Publishing.

Newman, Roberta L. *Keys to Quality in School-Age Care.* (Video and Viewer's Guide.) 1993. Self-published. Distributed by Summerwind Communications.

Scofield, Rich, editor. *Summer Program Tips, Strategies and Activities.* 2001. Nashville: School-Age NOTES.

Stassevitch, Verna, et al.. *Ready-to-Use Activities for Before and After School Programs.* 1998. West Nyack: Center for Applied Research in Education.

Wallace, Edna. *Summer Sizzlers and Magic Mondays: School-Age Theme Activities.* 1994. Nashville: School-Age NOTES.

Whitaker, David L. *Games, Games, Games: Creating Hundreds of Group Games and Sports.* 1996. Nashville: School-Age NOTES.

More resources on the following page...

Resources for Building on Your Skill as a School-Age Professional:

Aycox, Frank. *Games We Should Play in School.* 2nd edition. 1997. Discovery Bay: Front Row Experience.

Bailey, Dr. Becky. *There's Gotta Be A Better Way: Discipline That Works!* 1997. Oviedo: Loving Guidance, Inc.

Jones, Alanna. *Team-Building Activities for Every Group.* 1999. Richland: Rec Room Publishing.

Koralek, Derry, Roberta Newman and Laura Colker. *Caring for Children in School-Age Programs, Vols. 1 & 2.* 1995. Washington DC: Teaching Strategies.

Kreidler, William and Lisa Furlong. *Adventures in Peacemaking: A Conflict Resolution Activity Guide for School-Age Programs.* 1995. Cambridge: Educators for Social Responsibility.

Lawyer-Tarr, Sue. *School-Age Child Care Professional Training.* 1991. Midwest City: The Clubhouse.

Lewis, Barbara. *The Kid's Guide to Service Projects.* 1995. Minneapolis: Free Spirit Publishing.

Miller, Karen. *The Crisis Manual: How to Handle the Really Difficult Problems.* 1996. Beltsville: Gryphon House.

Newman, Roberta L. *Building Relationships with Parents and Families in School-Age Programs.* 1998. Nashville: School-Age NOTES.

Whelan, Mary Steiner. *But They Spit, Scratch and Swear! The Do's and Dont's of Behavior Guidance with School-Age Children.* 2000. Minneapolis: A-ha! Communications.

Find these and many other activity resource books at **School-Age NOTES**. Complete descriptions can be found at **www.AfterSchoolCatalog.com**.